River with an A

Christina Rivera

BookLeaf
Publishing

India | USA | UK

Presentation by *BookLeaf Publishing*

Web: www.bookleafpub.com

E-mail: info@bookleafpub.com

ISBN: 9789358318722

First edition 2023

DEDICATION

I dedicate this book to my students who have always loved me for the little things. May they remember not only my teachings but to also make most of their talents and to enjoy life as it comes, with all of it's adventures. I also dedicate this book to my people, the ones who always pushed me to publish my poems and never stopped believing in better tomorrows. I dedicate this book to myself and my little, may we always enjoy similar ways of life but may she be every bit the wiser and live it better than I.

ACKNOWLEDGEMENT

My very first teacher in middle school encouraged me to take upon a journalism class, that class bestowed in me a love for expressive writing and allowed me to have a healthy outlet for what would be an exhilarating lifestyle. In the years to follow, I would learn to utilize poetry as a way of escaping my inner most fears as well as expressing my deepest scars. It was my healthy digest of the world I lived in.

Cravings

Ever just want to scream and let it all out?
With one gush of air
Exhale, chaos.
Inhale, peace.

Ever just want to sprint and literally get lost?

With one step

Pace from familiarity and burst into the
unknown

Ever just want to dream and experience pure
serenity?
With one eye closed
  drift
      from
         reality
   Escape to Neverland

Ever just want to love and surrender your all?
With that one right person...
Let go of
 everything to
  receive even more.

Shadow Stitched Comforter

Stifling,
sickening words used to describe this bed.
One night of rest in it,
influenza starts to cripple you in dread.
Creeping out of desire what lackluster emotions
expelled
Twist, turn,
the bed bugs start to dance as they know well.
Beguiling words for love into melodious tunes
of capture
Promising notes of belonging is why you came,
but lust is what you're after.
Co-sleeping in the dust,
prideful ways undone.
Harboring a multitude of lies
Waking up to distasteful skies.

Final Destination

Have you ever sat in the dark so long,
you could almost see the light?
Walked for so long,
your feet were afraid of flight?
Took a trip outside to gaze upon the night sky,
Realized it had turned gray.

Reflections of a rainy day.

Soaking wet and still won't let your feet stop
marching.
Water rolling down your spine, a reminder that
the crowd is still watching.
Waiting for the day that you make your final
move.
Up out of the abyss into a sacred groove,
One of caring compassion not found amongst
this land.
The place where all others go and not just the
damned.

Amazing Grace

It's crazy how things happen.
Like how you see things before they occur,
And how your words mature.
Into being.
God you are so redeeming.
You realized the greatness in the sky before the
stars were placed.
Recognized my face before I was in this
airspace.

Angelic Apease

When her lips spelled out love I just
had to kiss her,
Allowed me to comfort her heart.
Let me ease her mind.
Remember all wounds heal with time.
Scars remain.
Remind us of the pain.
Gone are the days, gone are the days.
Far away.
Those were the days.

Naught For Nut

Scratching. Clawing. Crawling instead of words.
Our bodies verbs.
The weather is hell's defined perfection.
Nothing but melanin melting under the suns
reflections.

A Puzzling Pitch

Call me the jigsaw master
Everything I touch turns to pieces
One piece lets go, gives up and releases.
A lonely heart, cold, cracked but frozen creases.
To say a lover's touch could provide warmth...
An insane person's thesis.

Gestures of a Cheat

You show so much support for them,
their houses stand upon your stilts.
Putting time into healing all their wounds,
concealing scars with your shameless filth.
How do you find it fancified to galivant amongst
the jesters?
Words can only be justified when foolishness is
not in the answers.

Lust Lies Between Eyes

Its insane
I got you racked up on my brain
Cant stop looking crazy
Got my heart poured out
Like this bottle down the drain
Trickling to my destruction
With you is how i function
Disfunctionally functional in all of its abundance
Never trying to condence the meaningless sex
and gestures of your invitational eyes
Much to my surprise
I stumbled on a look
And fell on the hook between your legs
There is where I poured out much despair
And whispered for you to "take me there"
With no hesitation you galloped right in
Looked at me and said, "Let the games begin."
Delayed gratification, it was never thought
about.
Why buy frozen chicken just to thaw it out.
Now I'm sitting here wondering where my
mental could've been.
If we never were to have stumbled on the never
should've been.

Phantasmic First Love

A love so pure there is no one who can relate!
I hold you in my heart closer than the one who I
create.
God demands to put your husband first, for you
are my only mate.
I promise to abide by this and bring happiness
and more.
Days and nights spent away from you tear away
at my core.
To love and support you is what I will do.
My man, you are a dream come true.
In the night the moon shines brighter than the
sun,
I can be the darkness you help me overcome.
Push me towards greatness and carry me when
weak.
I never really thank you for helping me up the
creek.
You are the grass upon the hill,
I want to feel all your embrace.
I close my eyes and take a rolling dive to feel
you upon my face.
I can only hope you stain the clothes in which I
came to play.
Never intend to wash these threads,

I want you here to stay.
Make me filthy in your love, saturate my soul so
I am quenched.
If there ever be a drought,
I will rain dance till I am drenched.
I love you!

Construction of a Void

How come you dont make the heart feel like
home?
Neglecting my expressions of feeling alone.
The pain I cannot console
but to sit here and speak to walls of stone
which house eyes once warm now all acold
Numb to the plastures of different textures
Your wallpaper's cracks scream of different
pleasures
Declaring the importance of monetary measures
Importance of this completely over that
A battle once fought. No need to fight back.
How come you wont make this heart your
home?
Relay to me what touch fails to do
Build your home and make this heart anew.
One day, maybe, I might understand you
But for the ticks now and in between the tocks
Just love me stubbornly; don't never ever stop.

J.A.D.A

Looking at her smiling face,
With love the heart can never escape.
Jubilant days around her innocent ways.

Joyous
Anointed
Divinely
Adorable

Enlighten the whole world!
With her it's explorable.

Devil's Plunge

Left behind the masses,
just to play roulette with the dealer.
The bang was all too soft,
Now there's not much,
whom can heal her?

A Stenciled Massacre

15

You hurt me so bad my heart won't break,
Disintegrate.
Excavate my wounds with your icy smile.
Unearth the truths you've learned to beguile.
Sunken stupor
Accompanied abyss.
Your darkness filters my light with bliss.

A Beautiful Mind

A fanatic dreamer!
  Whisked away,
    by a fleeting
      thought.
  Accompanied by a reoccurring image.
  Floating on melodious memories,
  in route to the great timekeeper.

Just a pause,

  The hiccup
    that pushed
      against the clock's hands.
  Making way to disturb the gizmos and cogs,
  halting their seamlessly functional turning.

Love was a caterpillar.
  Alive in naive nature,
    unbeknownst to lurking dangers.
Inching afar across garden like acres.

Life flies like a butterfly.
  Whimsically floating from realistic to reality
  glimpsing at what could be.

Gliding from cocooned fragmented fantasies.
Giving way to a beautiful carefree life

Wonderland

It's a maze of cynical contortion
Make a left and see the straight
Proceed with caution to protect your fortune
For every turn decides your fate.
Right where I left it, the memory game
Flashes of days past perusing through tall grass.
Peekaboo of clarity, is that the way out?
Never mind, just another illusion
Water in a drought.

Psalms of God's Palms

You won't find me in no sacred place,
praying all my sins away.
I'll be dancing by the aquifer!
Amused by your streams,
A muse to my soul.
Dancing to the bird's chirps whistling songs of
stories untold.
Unhinge me with the whimsical wonder of your
nature,
allow me to lie down on blades of grass.
Soft'n the hardest rock; transform to sand.
Your hands is where my world began.

Pandora's Prey

Behind the brown drizzled in green,
I see the telling's of a million tingz.
A glance begets surface,
nothing to deep.
They fail to excavate her soul,
never to peep.
Flocks fly 'round and look no further.
Hunters pry to find no nurture.
Studious ones take time and set a gaze.
Wondering, wake minds glide through her maze.
Hinder none and yet foe & hero to few.
Her tormented soul bellows.
Who destroys who?

Foraging Friendship

Would you howl at the sun with me?
And together be wild things!
An uncanny mixture
Explicit insatiable flings!
Lead stubborn minds to wondering,
Let us not be explained!
Moreover, be an exploratory being.
Fight past temptation,
hold fast to patience.
Time begets a masterpiece upon a blank canvas.
Be the painter and I the brush.
Let's make magic and forge havoc!
Behold me and be my mirror.
Let's use each other's light to draw out figures.
Outline my smile with your gracious ways.
Let's see how long our friendship stays!

Shepard's Pie

Be wary of the camouflaged ewes,
grazing amongst the unbeknownst few...

Daily declaring deceitful disdain.
Enabling egotistical enamor.
Finessing friends for fools fain.
Generating guises growing grievous glamor.

Wolves don drip, sweating sensual sweet
fragrance.
Toxins seep,
sickening inhalers.
Creating laitance, a non-durable essence.
Be the tortoise, not the hare!
Hone your patience.
False pretense begets hatred.
Mindful of the one's who paved it.

Remedial Reflection

With one gaze in the mirror,
what do you see?
The sums of all my imperfections staring back at
me.
My nose too pointy, fat, or too rare.
I can never remove the kink from my hair.
Waist ain't slim enough,
booty too small.
Breasts no longer sit,
all
   they do
        is fall.
Negativity clings like the hair on my skin.
Never fleeing just swaying in the wind.
What other's see I have trouble finding.
Hiding in plain sight,
amuse to unwind me.
Search and never finding,
looking to never find.
A gaze in the mirror,
can last a lifetime.

www.ingramcontent.com/pod-product-compliance
Lightning Source LLC
LaVergne TN
LVHW010857200726

843508LV00012B/2924